Created by Pendleton Ward

Written by **Ashly Burch**

Illustrated by **Diigii Daguna**

Colours by **Braden Lamb**

Letters by **Warren Montgomery**

Cover by **Braden Lamb & Shelli Paroline**

"Fish Days"
Written & Illustrated by Marina Julia

With Special Thanks to Marisa Marionakis, Janet No, Nicole Rivera, Conrad Montgomery, Meghan Bradley, Curtis Lelash, Kelly Crews and the wonderful folks at Cartoon Network.

ISLANDS

ADVENTURE TIME: ISLANDS
ISBN - 9781785861222

ADVENTURE TIME: ISLANDS, February 2017. Published by Titan Comics, a division of Titan Publishing Group Ltd., 144 Southwark St., London, SE1 0UP. ADVENTURE TIME, CARTOON NETWORK, the logos, and all related characters and elements are trademarks of and © Cartoon Network. (S16) All rights reserved. All characters, events and institutions depicted herein are fictional. Any similarity between any of the names, characters, persons, events and/or institutions in this publication to actual names, characters, and persons, whether living or dead and/or institutions are unintended and purely coincidental.

A CIP catalogue record for this title is available from the British Library.

Printed in China.

10 9 8 7 6 5 4 3 2 1

SSSH~

Ftt

TOM!

Strum

strum

CAN'T SLEEP AGAIN, HUH, JO? WAS IT BAD BEANS OR BAD DREAMS?

HAHA, GROSS!

BAD DREAMS. THERE WAS THIS HUGE SNAKE GUY AND HE NABBED ME. NOW MY HEAD WON'T STOP BUZZIN'. WHAT DO YOU DO WHEN YOUR HEAD WON'T STOP BUZZIN'?

WELL, I FIND THE BEST MEDICINE FOR HEAD BUZZIN' IS TO PLAY THE GUITAR SO LOUD THAT YOU CAN'T EVEN HEAR YOURSELF THINK.

EASY THERE, KIDDO. YOU'RE ALL RIGHT.

grm

GOOD THING MARCY TAUGHT YOU HOW TO SWIM, HUH?

...PLEASE DON'T LEAVE.

HE'S GONNA GET AWAY!

ACTUALLY...WE'D BETTER GET THESE BERRIES BACK TO YOUR BROS. THAT VAMP DUDE CAN WAIT.

I'LL PACK 'EM UP!

HOW 'BOUT A PATENTED MARCELINE MUD PIE?

HA HA! EW! NO WAY!

I WISH WE COULD MAKE A PIE OUTTA THESE.

READY... AIM...!

FIIIRRREEE-

FH

FWOMP

FFT

Slap

MORNIN', KIDDO! YOU'RE UP EARLY. GET A LOT OF PEELING DONE?

HA HA, UM, YEAH. HOW COME NOBODY'S ON THE UPPER DECK?

WHERE WERE YOU EVEN AIMING, WYATT?!

Pffft

I THINK EVERYONE'S JUST, UH, TAKING THEIR TIME GETTIN' UP THERE TODAY, IS ALL. WANT A SANDWICH?

LISTEN, JO...I KNOW YESTERDAY WAS A SCARY DAY. BUT NOTHIN' LIKE THAT IS GONNA HAPPEN AGAIN. I PROMISE. DO YOU BELIEVE ME?

UM...

TOM!

YOU HAVE TO COME LOOK!
IT'S--WE--JUST COME
LOOK!!

GASP

VAMPIRES? THAT GRIZZ IS REAL? MAN. WE HAD SOME WEIRD SLUDGE GUYS. NO VAMPIRES, THOUGH. MOSTLY IT WAS JUST REALLY HOT.

BUT LIKE, THE TOO-HOT-TO-LIVE KIND OF HOT.

HEY EVERYBODY, I GOT SOMETHIN' TO SAY.

SOUNDS PRETTY CHOICE TO ME.

YEEEEEEY~

SLOSH

YO, JO!

COME CLIMB THIS TREE WITH ME!

UH... OKAY!

HIYA TOM!

HEY! SEE ANYTHING GOOD FROM UP THERE?

NOPE! GUESS WE'LL JUST HAVE TO GO HIGHER!

NIGHT BERRIES...

MARCY! WHAT WOULD MARCY DO?

PROBBO EAT SOME OF THESE GUYS. YOU HUNGRY?

WHOA, YEAH.

GRUMBLE

pfft

MUNCH

NOW WHAT?

WELL... WHAT DO YOU WANNA DO?

I WANNA GO HOME. I WANNA SEE TOM.

WHICH WAY IS HOME?

I DON'T KNOW! I DON'T EVEN KNOW WHERE I AM!

THERE'S AN EASY WAY TO FIND OUT.

MARCY,
IT'S THE
WINDMILL!
I CAN SEE THE
WINDMILL!

I KNOW
WHICH
WAY TO
GO!

STAY AWAY MON STERS!

Rustle

Rustle

GASP

BOOP

BAD SNAKEY. I DON'T WANNA FIGHT YOU.

SHOO!

?

NICE ONE, BUNS.

THANKS, FOR HELPING ME GET THROUGH THIS.

HEY, MARCY?

YEAH?

AM I EVER GONNA SEE YOU AGAIN?

OH JO, IT WAS ALL MY FAULT. MY CARELESSNESS...I HAD GOTTEN YOU...

I KNEW I COULDN'T LOSE ANYONE ELSE AGAIN.

SO I GOT SOME OF OUR BRAINIER FOLKS TO DESIGN THIS GUY! I'M CALLING IT 'THE GUARDIAN.' DO YOU LIKE THE NAME? I'M STILL WORKSHOPPING IT.

WHAT'S IT...DO?

IT'LL DEFEND US! IT'LL GO AROUND THE ISLAND, WHAM-BLAMMING ANYTHING THAT MOVES. WE'LL HAVE THIS PLACE ALL TO OURSELVES! WHADAYA THINK?

TOM... YOU CAN'T DO THAT.

WHY NOT?

The End...

IT'S VERY BAD LUCK NOT TO NAME YOUR FISH.

MMMMM ISN'T THAT FOR BOATS?

I THINK IT'D BE RUDE NOT TO NAME THEM.

GUSTO, THE LEADER!

PEGLEG, THE BEST DANCER!

CINDER, THE SASSY ONE!

AND... SANDRA DEE.

THE SHY ONE.

FISH DAYS TIP #2
GOLDFISH NEED A
BIG TANK!

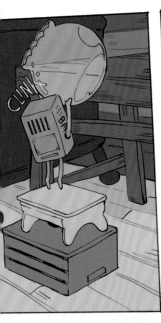

BOWLS ARE
TOO SMALL!

FISH DAYS TIP #3
FOOD THAT SINKS IS BETTER
FOR THEM THAN FLOATING
FISH FLAKES!

OOF.

EAT UP,
LITTLE ONES!

CREAK

SPLISH
SPLISH
SPLISH
SPLISH

BUT NOT *TOO* COLD,

FISH DAYS

SHIVER

SCOOP SCOOP

FISH DAYS TIP #6

CHANGE THE WATER OFTEN AND CIRCULATE AIR INTO THE TANK!

JUST FOR YOU!

PHEEEEWW

HMMM

UH...

SO HOW LONG DO I HAVE TO DO THIS?

DON'T STOP!

FISH DAYS TIP# 7
WHEN TAKEN CARE OF
THE RIGHT WAY,
GOLDFISH CAN LIVE A
LONG TIME AND GROW
UP REAL BIG!

END